THE SWAMP MONSTER AT HOME

POEMS

Catherine Carter

THE SWAMP MONSTER AT HOME

LOUISIANA STATE UNIVERSITY PRESS)|(BATON ROUGE

Published by Louisiana State University Press
Copyright © 2012 by Catherine Carter
All rights reserved
Manufactured in the United States of America
LSU Press Paperback Original

DESIGNER: *Mandy McDonald Scallan*
TYPEFACE: *Minion*

Library of Congress Cataloging-in-Publication Data

Carter, Catherine, 1967–

The swamp monster at home : poems / Catherine Carter.
    p. cm.
ISBN 978-0-8071-4280-6 (pbk. : alk. paper) — ISBN 978-0-8071-4281-3 (pdf) — ISBN 978-0-8071-4282-0
(epub) — ISBN 978-0-8071-4283-7 (mobi)
I. Title.
PS3603.A7769S93 2012
811'.6—dc23

2011030089

Grateful acknowledgment is made to the editors of the following publications, in which the poems listed
appeared previously, sometimes in slightly different form: *Asheville Poetry Review:* "The Book of Steve" (as
"Adam and Steve"); *Best American Poetry 2009:* "The Book of Steve"; *Connotations:* "The Hole" and "Mid-July,
39"; *Cortland Review:* "Legacy" and "One More Ars Poetica"; *Fugue:* "Maytide: The Orgy"; *Louisville Review:*
"The Body"; *The Lyric:* "Hydro Plant Accommodates Rafting Industry" and "Losing the Way"; *Marjorie Kin-
nan Rawlings Journal of Florida Literature:* "Sprickets," "Leaffall," and "That Time Again"; *North Carolina
Conversations:* "Hook Woman"; *North Carolina Literary Review:* "Eggcorns" and "In the Graveyard"; *Orion:*
"The Dawn of Time"; *Ploughshares:* "Arson in Ladytown"; *Raintown Review:* "Men's Neckties"; *Redheaded
Stepchild:* "The Earthquake"; *Snowy Egret:* "This Time." "Among the Assassins" first appeared in the chap-
book *The Lowly, Exalted*, published by the University of Southern Maine in conjunction with its "Spineless
Wonders" exhibition in 2009.

for Brian

Contents

THE SWAMP MONSTER AT HOME

The Dawn of Time

It had always been twilight
and it would always be twilight, God's
hour or the dinosaurs' or, more
likely, just the sweet unending
amoeba's, as each split itself
off from the original and eternal
cell: one myriad amoeba
on the rocking sea-face
and the faint glint of stars
never setting, circling
the pole like a bear's hip,
a water wheel. Then,
change. Then
some primordial ape-animal
standing out on the sandy
cape of forever looked over
her shoulder and said,
in her clumsy grunt,
"yesterday . . . "
She didn't know what she had
started. Probably she only
meant to say, "yesterday
was like today," but it was enough.
The sea began to heave.
The endless twilight began
to end, peeling westward
like stripped skin. The stars
covered their eyes as the new
thing dragged up
its bloody, fiery crown
from the deep. Gears clashed
in the brightening air, deadlines
for reports began to pour
in, atoms everywhere synchronized

their watches for millennia
of slow, precise decay,
as out at the rim of every
thing, never to set
or stop again, time dawned
into the ticking day.

The Book of Steve

"God made Adam and Eve, not Adam and Steve."

But what if God did? What if I showed you
the lost book in that cramped hand some call Moses',
right to left (you read Hebrew, right?), the Book of Steve?
Stefan, if you're Orthodox, Esteban
if you also love the Virgin of Guadalupe,
but never mind those dark madonnas. The Book of Steve:
much like the rest of the Pentateuch, you'll recognize
the style, except that it was before Genesis 1
when Steve became a living soul. A lively, friendly soul:
when those animals came questing, Steve was thrilled.
He scratched their ears as he named them, pulled
their ticks, asked them what they thought they should be called.
So he was scratching and chatting, naming away,
when up came Adam (Yahweh had been practicing men).
"Hey, dude." "Hey, Adam. You think this looks
like a crocodile?" "I dunno. More like a fox?"
They had a few beers (Yahweh's work of the day),
named five kinds of ants: Steve got carpenter,
leaf-cutter, sugar; Adam took fire and soldier.
Probably they made love, probably a lot (the world
was young then), but the Book of Steve is demure;
Moses, or someone, drew the curtain of discretion.

When the curtain comes up, the snake
still has brief feet, but Adam is changing the names
to better ones, and Steve's not there. It seems
there were complaints. Steve talked too much, always on
about feelings, food, the slant of the light; sometimes
he wanted to be on top; he took the remote, and didn't
give it back when Adam glared. And his chest wasn't nearly
enough like a pillow. It was all too much.

The end of the book is torn out; there are marks of fire.
No one knows who defiled the Book of Steve,
but in some stories it is said that Eden has other quadrants
and that Steve is in one of them.
Steve, and the snakes with feet, and other people
who missed the next book: the roc preening its iridescent plumes,
the unicorn lipping apples, the manticore having a dustbath.
They say that among the leaves of western Eden
was found a helpmeet for Steve, who was not fruitful,
who did not multiply, who had no dominion over the earth.

Arson in Ladytown

I hate Ladytown—so much can go wrong down there.

—STEPH

Things weren't looking good in Ladytown.
True, it was always lush, like D.C. in August,
high humidity, but that year the very
brickwork sweated salt. That year
the metro chafed the tunnel walls and the train
whistles' wail rose to a new pitch
of dismay, for that year there was to be
a procedure, proceeding God knew where.
And if you thought you had troubles before—
those eerie white fungi, the quakes
that wrung blood from the stones of the streets—
well. Now the arched gates were pried open
with steel rams. Now came the burning,
like misogynistic madmen were firing
the curtains and laying down flammables
in the bookstores and gardens and coffeeshops
of Ladytown, shuddering the muscular
silky foundations. Eggs scrambled themselves
on the shimmering asphalt. Ambulances
screamed in, flames licked and leapt from bramble
to billboard to hospital to house, men
fled clutching babies and books and balls.
It's easy to get tired of a city someone
is burning around you. Easy to wish the town
would just get up and move,
no matter how it happened. Even the women
wished they lived somewhere else,
though there was nowhere for them to go,
all that blistering summer in Ladytown.

Some Kisses

The feet are promiscuous. They kiss the worn
bluegreen boards of the porch with long love,
and the blisterdrops of gold sap crushed up
from the wood, those are only more kisses,
hot ones. But they also kiss the whispering
fescue; running water makes them shiver.
Long ago they swore to be true
to the fine sand of tidewater, black and white,
but the sand knew they lied. Maybe
it forgave them; sand too will sift in anywhere,
press itself to anyone. They grow more
and more passionate as they lose
the leathery soles they grew as young feet,
as the earth hurts them harder and they flinch
every time, but keep coming back for one more
sole kiss. Tonight they remember their wilder days;
tonight they'd go out again in bad company,
black asphalt, glittering with shattered glass.
Tonight they don't mind if the kiss ends in blood.

The Goddess Freyja in the E.R.

for Ulrike

Why it should be Freyja
I didn't know then; it might have been
Brigid (darker, hands shining with fire),
or Demeter (that rye-fair hair),
but she was Swedish and beautiful,
a blessing from shores
of Vikings and porn: that
doctor we most needed,
right then, unlikely as grace,
glowing like grain, strode through
a swaying door to put her hand
into my love's hair, touch his broken
head (he said
he felt more than just pain
just then), tell him he wasn't
so broken after all, choke
on her soda when he told her
the silly way he'd been hurt. And
(crossing the parking lot, safe
again in the lucky world
I knew) I thought, *Freyja*. For Freyja,
suzerain of love, rules too
the souls of half the fallen, the raven-
reaping of those wasteful wars.
She is goddess of long wave-
steeds and brave men, the opal-
blaze in the long end-
cold, apotheosis come to show us
the host-filled hall at the end
of fear, to give us
what we couldn't deserve, to tell me
Ragnarok was not yet here.

That Time Again

When I wake in the black
early morning, the morning
star is Saturn, burning
yellow and steady in the window's
icewater square like a warning
flare. You lumber toward the shower
and returning day, while in the winter
night Saturn and I
stare at each other, wary,
cold as two diamonds.
You have left your shirt
on the quilt, its warmth
turning thin in the chill.
After a while I lean
out stealthy and quick and catch
it under the cover by its collar,
hide it against my side
where Saturn won't see.

The Pack

It's August out there. The broad canopies, still
dusty green under the sun, are gray in the dark,
katydid-loud under the gibbous moon
where the deep baying has begun. In each
dog-day noon, the jewelweed leaves
droop and hang limp, awaiting shade.
This is not the time for these dogs
to come tracing and coursing up the road,
across the yard, back and forth, seizing sleep
and peace in their tense jaws and shaking
them like some doomed hare. The stardog
doesn't rise till late September, the wild
hunt won't ride till the leaves fall.
We knew they'd be coming,
the black poodle down the valley
belling faint and clear, the rib-
deep yell of the rufous bloodhound
attuned to the bass of our sweat, no
matter how still we huddle in our summer
sheets, the silent hound to whom the moon
shadows lend two extra heads;
but not yet. This is too soon to hear
that steady, deadly song, this isn't right,
it's not time yet, not here at summer's prime.

Cast Casing, Eastern Pondhawk

Ribbed as a workboat's close-lapped strakes,
six splayed claws clasping the frond where it crawled
up out of its years as water-lurker, worm-scourge,
the broad brown casing crisps in the sun, abandoned
as the spired cathedral when the converted have slipped
away to the high hill for the forbidden fires,
the leap of May Day, the sacrifice-
meat and the dance of desire. Flesh out of flesh
struggled, damp, teneral, vulnerable
from the murk, and now the flesh
has gone. The cast caul hangs
like an alien, armored, indifferent, while the thing
itself sings out over water, one with the world
we recognize: green metallic face, great
terrible eyes, bunting-blue needle-shine mail,
and spot-gauze, blot-gauze wings that make
the predator's streaming authorial lines
of movement and force, of certainty, savage speed
and innocent greed—
skeeterhawk, snake doctor, devil's darner,
flash and ravage of the air, joy of the summer ponds.

Sump

You don't know it, but
there's a crack in the cellar floor.
At first it seems as though the flow
just seeps in, ambient,
but it's that crack, that flaw
from tens of years back, a tiny steady
bubble from saturated sand, trickling
downhill over the bumpy floor to the sump
hole. Sump water begins to swell, microns
at a time, invisible to the eye, but all
the way up to the shingle
roof you can feel it
filling. Up and up, licking
harsh walls with its thin black tongue.
The sump hole is a well of souls:
down there are dead mouse, fallen
sparrow, drowned toad, endless
camel crickets, still whole
with anaerobic decay, all
all but liquid in their skins.
It rains and rains.
Foul silver creeps across
concrete, wells toward the wires.
The sump pump stammers, chokes.
In the well, corpses start to stir;
the water shivers. It is coming
and you can't bail enough; you can't
drain it out; nothing
you can do will stop it now.

Losing the Way

You know how, when the sun slides into cloud,
the whole woods change their angles, and you're lost
in trees you've known forever? they fade gray,
the vivid glittering mosses sink to rust,
and even the river that will lead you down
to someplace known seems to have turned around
and run upstream, as if to feed the seeps
that shrink in a dry season. All the wood
is hardly forty acres, counting in
the plots on either side that never were
your own in truth; but when the sun has gone
under, it is trackless, shadowless,
it might go on forever. And your home
might have become some twilit fairy wood
where everyone you know grows old outside
while you drink with inhuman hosts who never
recall your name, or where it is you're from.

Today it happened: the unstraying path,
which at the best of times is more a ghost
of old log-roads that hacked the ground, has crossed
(while I looked) over to oblivion
and thinned and vanished like a cloud of breath.
I know somewhere to rightward is the river
west-running toward the bay-coast where it means
to be, tomorrow nightfall, and that means
that somewhere leftward is the path to where
I trusted I'd get back. The tall trees' bones,
stripped by winter, glimmer in the cloud-
light that bleaches papery leaves like frost.
I say now, half-aloud, "It must be close . . ."

But from the sloughs and hollows of the woods,
no answer; it's as if the very ground
that for so many years has quivered up
into my feet has fallen finally mute,
and in the woods where I knew every branch
like family, I find I'm lost at last.

Mid-July, 39

Mid-July, high
noon, everything still but the flicker
of wind, the soft roar
from the chilling buildings.
Sun hot at my back, shade
a short bar thrown forward
from my feet. The white
birch, slimmer than any
girl I was, scatters single brown
pennies, oblong, thin. The willow's
yellow leaves, sparse among
the green, are twisted
like carnival ribbons;
when they fall, they flutter
wildly: sudden fevers,
party favors.
Forsyth Hall's
generator throbs. The green
birch leaves glitter.
I sit a second longer
in the middle, fallow,
hollow, still
here at the center, heat
beating up from the earth, summer
wind going toward winter.

Hook Woman

The story wasn't real.
It scared you anyway:
kids groping in the car, then roaring away,
bloody hook rattling the handle.
If you'd had any chance of getting
any, that hook might even
have deterred you; as it was,
you were just scared
to cross the dark parking lot
at your safe school, to hike
your empty road at night
and watch the dangerous moon
climbing the thin trees, the long field:
you'd be attacked, hacked,
hooked. You wouldn't go that way
once evening turned on daylight's hinge,
and shadow cracked
your sureties like the line of black
made by a door ajar, a cellar door
with down and dark behind.

At forty, almost sure
no hook-handed madmen lurked
by brook or branch, you took
a glass of brandy, rolled on
a sweater, strolled down your hill
and up the next through
the stripy shadows of the gibbous
moon, watching Cygnus
sprawl up the sky, the stars
of autumn caught
in dry trees. But in a cold pool

of backward and uncanny light,
the white glimmer caught the glass in your hand,
and there on your shadow's black
arthritic wrist was a swan's
head, a cane's crook-handle, or
(you knew it now) a hook. Now
it's you who prowl the road by night,
strike fear into children waiting
to make out in the backs
of cars. It's been there
all along on your hand
where it always belonged,
awaiting the dangerous moon
to make it shine like bone.

The Earthquake

This wasn't earthquake country.
The world was sound and still,
a great turtle sleeping for peaceful
decades on the sunny sea
of everything else. Here marriages
endured; children were safe
from their parents; long
labor was enough. Here things
seemed what they were.

Nor was it like the books, the places
where the earth rippled and bucked, stood up
and shook off its chains. This was the dark
of the morning, five o'clock, an awakening
to vibration: steady, soft, a buzz
or a hum, a tremor like the first faint
signatures of nerve disease.

But I knew, though it took
sleepy moments to recall. I knew
that under these hard mountains ran a fault.
I knew that though no one could see
the break, the alteration, everything
for years ahead would change. I sat up
and reached out my hand to feel
that deep soft shaking of the walls.
I said *earthquake,* and I named that fault,
I took it for my own.

"Have a Blessed Day"

Hard to know what they mean
when they wish you a blessed day:
a day your boss is kind,
when you manage not to say
anything really dumb?
a day when you don't get
diagnosed with herpes?
or when you don't forget
your own name, or don't catch
a cold that lasts three weeks?
It's hard to know. A blessing,
maybe, isn't change,
and isn't really luck, but joy:
the world goes shy and strange
in some transforming light
on what's already here—

as today, when I turned
in my unsteady chair,
incredulous, and someone
I hadn't thought to see
at all, this whole year,
stood there. He spoke to me;
he'd come to speak to me.
Nothing I knew would say
itself; but liking rose
around us—the everyday
walls quivered like bright water;
the air went deep as wine.
I don't know that he felt
that shimmer in the spine
as I did; but I did.
It was enough, that lift
of blood, that benediction:
the blessed day's unasked gift.

Hydro Plant Accommodates Rafting Industry

"LAND OF MANY USES"

—SIGN FOR THE NANTAHALA NATIONAL FOREST

All the long drive upstream,
the rocks were knobby-dry,
the stream lay sullen, low and slow,
in broken symmetry,

its mortal bones exposed.
Its quivering, glinting flesh
was gone to feed the power grid,
its slender nervous fish

cringing in too-warm pools.
But as we came downstream,
we saw the whitewater revive,
the thirsty, dusty brim

go under in the rise,
the gleam, the hurrying foam
and steady surge of weight and strength
as captive water came,

released, downstream. And we—
my slow car and I—kept
pace with the sparkling, moving line
of current as it crept

downstream to raise the creek
for weekend rafters to
make use of the commodity
of river. It would go

on to the reservoir
whose banks were forty feet
above where they had always stood
in the ongoing drought.

The temporary flood
was short as autumn love,
with months of dust on either side
no torrent could remove,

but lit the day as love will.
Briefly the stream put on
its spangled flesh to resurrect
the shrunken skeleton.

Torch Song

Don't ask how long I've carried this torch,
through how many goldenrods and purple
ironweeds I've borne its burning crown,
how many rue anemone and foam-
flowers its flickering sparks have stung.
I'm ashamed to say. It's a lot.
Often enough I've tucked it under
an arm to have the use of both hands,
half dropped it, snatched it back,
scorching an underarm or thigh,
threatening grainfields and barns.
Sometimes I've held it high
as I can, scattering liquid tar
and hot pitch as a dragon might fling
flaming spittle, searing freckles
onto shoulder and forearm. Don't
ask how long I can hold onto this;
I won't promise you a thing.
There'd be little surprise in looking back
over my spotted shoulder to find
a few decades behind, or the judgment
day suddenly at hand. Or I might
lay it down anytime. Tomorrow.
Next week. I can only say
I haven't done it yet. It won't be today.

Sneakthief

When I saw you again,
I had been stealing grains of meal,
rancid bones, making do so long
I hardly felt it any more.
But now. Now a wealth
of words bulged your pockets, gold
ran from your hands, I saw my chance,
itched to work this trade again. You
were shining-rich, Midas-bright,
and you didn't even know! Oh,
easy mark, how my hands twitched,
how my mouth watered:
this was my work and I loved it.

I sidled close. I felt your soft
voice in the air, fixed my eyes
on the turn of your hands, glanced away
as often as I dared, feared
someone must see what I wanted,
yes, and what I took. First your sharp
eyes, your bright bones, that smile like
sweet cocaine; then a deft hand dipped
in the pocket where you hide
kindness, joy, wit, before I snatched
at the sleeve of your coat, and ran. I half-
expected the cry to rise, *Stop!*
thief! And yet, relief! no one
called, no one saw my arms strain
to hold twenty-year scotch,
your grandmother's gold leaf, small true
Bose speakers anyone would covet.
I dragged back your hoard

(spilled coins flashing
after), tumbled it to the table,
snatched up the pen, let
stolen desire run up into the hand
and out in the ink. I stole
what I had to have, I got
what I wanted from you.

The Kings of Tarshish

... for love is a most receiving thing, as anyone can attest who has
been loved without returning it. It is the one who is loved who must
give and give.

—THEODORE STURGEON, "THE SILKEN-SWIFT"

The kings of Tarshish and of the isles shall bring presents: the kings
of Sheba and Seba shall offer gifts.

—PSALMS 72:10

Like a workboat going out on the face
of the waters, with the morning
turning and flashing in the churn
and the wash pulling to the surface
the foil flicker of minnows
and shrimp, each love brings everything
back in his wake, everything
else, everything you've forgotten
to see in the press of the days.
It's like Christmas was, before you knew
the time had come to pass that on to the young.
Like the kings of Tarshish, he brings gifts.
The Gloucestershire Wassail chiming all day
in some harpsichord under your skin.
Live crabs streaming bright baywater,
cerulean claws knobbed with cutting ivory,
tipped and jointed with scarlet,
and borne to you to be released, not eaten.
The thin moon curving up the lambent sky,
virgin again, every time—
you wonder he has time for anything,
when he's so busy bearing these to you!
To hold them all, you too grow brighter,
deeper, redeemed for today at least

from violence and deceit. They make you want
to thank him (though you can't);
they make you celebrate again
all love's unknowing offerings.
Though you were made to take them, and you do,
they make you wish you too could give and give.

Maytide: The Orgy

Their bodies may be made
of fossil light, but today the blades
and ovals and palms of the leaves
are drinking their meal fresh
from the sun, like some great mild
cow, and the milk none the worse
for running ninety-three
million miles. And with the sweets
(how human) comes love:
even the elms blush at sugar,
flush gold, and wave their fingers
in its sweet rush. It is
promiscuous and innocent, excessive
and splendid, the love-in
of these people who lip the sun
like syrup, whose sap runs
with it. It is a great
tumble and splash, a chaos
of desire and delight; the pinks bathe
in the passion of oaks,
the doghobbles' semeny blooms
mingle with peonies.
Spilling lace, pouring dust
and breath, gone gold with light,
the trees are making love
everywhere, all day, all night.

With Child

That April morning the roof ripped
itself loose in a wild swirl of wind.
Maybe a witch went by, riding the cyclone,
but you can't be sure, you were so busy
scrambling: would it freeze tonight,
would you ever sleep again,
what about your work? Slowly
the wind fell and
fell until the air was still
and the dust motes came
into being and began to shimmer like summer
midges. Maybe it was the early sun,
creeping down the rock edges
into the valley. Maybe
it was just the pause in the roofless walls
of generation, the shades
of ancestors wandering through,
continuing after all.
You knew you'd never again have a roof,
you'd spend your years shivering with terror
and brief delight, the floor
would be treacherous mud,
the ceiling the fierce
wheel of constellations.
You panicked and hoped,
made lists and plans all
month long, till the morning you woke
in the chill to the seep of blood
and the hammers firing.
It was over. You were safe.
Carpenters' shadows shut the light
as the roof came down again
like the lid of some long box,
nail by nail by nail.

Haggadah

after the miscarriages

I tried to be slave;
you can't blame anyone
if you do it yourself,
and I tried. If I'd had
my way, I'd have died there.
Nor do I know even now
whose was the whisper bidding
Pharoah let me go. But I have gone:
answered, the prayers I wouldn't speak;
painted with gore, the doorposts
I won't enter again. Salt stains
everything when I count
the cost, and the lost: tender
frogs shriveling on highways, cattle
lowing bitterly as the sores spread,
kinder masters who didn't know
what they asked, the firstborn
and the unborn. But you,
whoever you are, you
have given me back a free
woman's word and work,
a soul to make as I can,
and I can say only
praise. The dusty manna,
the pottage of lentils,
are sweeter than cucumber, catfish, melon,
now when you have brought me out of Egypt.

To the Unborn

That act that pries us out
of the mortal and into twenty
eternal seconds: it asks in
spirits. Spasm of cells and
convulsion of blood brought you,
sojourner from the endless
atomic now, into
the human house, its muscled
walls, its beating clocks. Incarnation,
you tried mortality, milk
and bread, wine and death,
before turning back to wild,
where sometime we may meet you
again, entirely changed. You had been
cloud and calcium. Argon and rain.
What would keep you in here
as that tailed tadpole, that gilled
grain of flesh? Apparently
nothing. We would
have carried you to the river
to help you remember;
perhaps you did; you were out
that door again quick
as half a word. We would
have lifted the sashes,
let the wind wash through,
so you might feel at home
here for a while. The last
time, when it was clear you never
would, I put what was left
out on the railing
where the crows come to feed,

and did feed. By nightfall
you were gone, taken up
by black beaks thick as a finger,
sharp as hunger: turned
back to nitrogen, heat,
twenty seconds' flight
inside those bright black wings,
more their kin than you were ever mine.

Sprickets

for Chesney, and her sprickets

Somewhere underneath the bright
reality, the titmice at the feeder, the holy
crows bullying and baying the sacred
owl and both coming back alive, there's that other
world, where the crickets look like spiders,
spiders that hop, all joints and prickles
and terrible bristles—call them sprickets.
In that world the crickets—not content with being
alive in a world that also holds your clean
wash surging on the line in the racketing
wind of March—the sprickets eat flesh.
Snaptrap a mouse and leave it huddled there
a few days, and they will pick its eyes
right out of its soft head. Very likely, if
you had some falling seizure where they lair,
the sprickets would pick the eyes
right out of your soft head. It wouldn't be
personal, but in the thick of such a world,
some life seems so alien you can only know
it through the soles, know only from that crunch
and squelch what you both share (death,
revulsion, hunger. Fear.).
And that world, maybe it's right
below the honey-toned hardwood, maybe
it's in your cellar. Maybe that world is here.

Sam and Ralph

In the cartoons the wolf
and the sheepdog have lunch
together. It's like the Christmas truce,
but the workday war is only
eight hours out of twenty-four.
Then the shriek of the whistle,
the clang of the clock:
the wolf adjusts his eyebrows
to indicate menace, lifts a lip
for a sparkle of fang, his bloodshot
eyes take on their yellow gleam again
as he slinks through the shrubbery,
and Sam the sheepdog snatches
Ralph by the neck and begins
shaking and pummeling like the terrible
guardian he is, like a wolf
himself. When five o'clock comes
the canids slouch wearily home
together one more day.
Like wrestling fans, the sheep never seem
to wonder about dog and wolf, Hacksaw
Duggan and Sergeant Slaughter
sharing beer after the match,
just doing their jobs.
They never ask what's in those
sandwiches, could it be lamb.
When the whistle stops
the relentless clock, even if Ralph limps
away wearing a dramatic sling,
it's always a beautiful sunset
for dog and wolf. Sam says,
you work too hard, Ralph, take tomorrow off.
I can handle both jobs.

November Evening, Splitting Stovewood

A neighbor drones his leaves away
with a leafblower, another combs
his with a rasping rake, while in my leaves
I stand ankle-deep, braced to the slow
swing of the axe. The damp heavy logs
are splotched bright with fungal jelly
like orange marmalade, like flesh if flesh
were the color of goldfish. Witches' butter:
in old stories it means a hex.
Maybe I'll scoop it off the log,
spread it on my neighbors' toast,
act for the lost leaves.
Maybe there'll be a golden quiver, an alien
taste, and then leaves
sifting over their quiet bodies,
slowly covering them under. But I
am the only witch here now,
writing dark thoughts
on the dry paper that whispers
under my soles, changing cold weight
and wood into heat, into light the color
of witches' butter.

There Is a Tide

Some huge seafloor moon-dragon sighs
in, the shoreline swells out, and where your keel
floated light in its shallow cove, now it grates
on grit, aground. It's a shock
at first; try as you will to shove and lever
and slide that boat, you won't be off for five
hours more. There's nothing you can do; that is,
you can set a stake to see if the tide's still gliding
out (it is), or despair, curse your own
careless pride that got you here, but it keeps sinking
away, creating fresh sand islands anew
to your ungrateful eyes. There's nothing you can do
save be glad it's a shady island, not some blistering
mudbar, no greenhead flies, the beer
and sandwiches in your cooler still all right.
Maybe, inside, you're not glad yet,
till it lifts in your mind like a hull
on waves: *there's nothing you can do.*
You can peer every nine minutes at your watch, perform
minute calculations how high it'll have to rise,
shove at it with your mind: come on, come
on, come *on.* It won't. You can give up and nap
under a high-tide bush, chase tiger beetles flitting
over the sand. You can circumnavigate your island
by wading, or braving the Lyme ticks of the deer-
browsed interior, and while you do it you can go
fast or slowly, look at anything you want to,
sit down and stare at the bright water-miles:
it doesn't matter. You'll go when it's time,
back to your regular hours, reports
hammered out by artificial light, inside. You'll go
when it's time, and the tide will tell you when

it's time. Until it is, there's nothing you can do
but be right where you are right now, see
what there is to see: green-throated lavender
oxalis, brown and white ospreys beating
through the pines and whistling their urgent
kee-kee-kee, the cormorants drying their wings.
You're at the mercy of tide, and its mercy
is surprisingly wide: until it's time, you're free.

Occult Bat Encounters

They're the meetings you don't know you've had,
maybe dreaming, one way or another:
with silent furred families laired in your roofbeams,
a caught bat wheeling through sleeping rooms.
You may see a barbed shadow flitter and dip,
but if it bit you, you won't know
till too late, the skinprick so delicate
no marks bleed or show.

And you are the encounters I never had
except half-asleep, the bites that came
to madness, or to nothing at all.
You, and you, and you—
occult meeting, mammal to mammal,
black as a cauldron,
secret as vodoun,
deep as a vault, obscure as guilt.

Toast

Here's to a man like the swoop and rise of an electric line.
At a distance he's some anonymous steel tower
stalking across the hillside, but come nearer
and you can't miss the power
vibrating through him. It could toast your skin
like bread. At ten feet he's no great beauty,
but at six the room gets warmer.
At four feet the heat's banked, a dormant ruby,
and you don't get to three. Maybe you're not the electrical kind;
maybe you like beeswax candles, the snap of woodfire,
maybe you've your own fire at home,
lively and hot. But there's that wire,
thrumming with acquiescence and resistance,
singing with force, lighting up streets.
Stripped of whatever insulates him, he'd fry
mountainsides; his tie-knot crisps with heat;
in November, rattlesnakes lair in his desk.
One day a condor tangled in his wiry hair;
it didn't end well. You wouldn't like being locked to that grid,
hooked in by manmade power. But the shimmering air
around him buzzes, fidgets, seethes, kinetic;
it takes some doing to resist the field
pulling your hand that way, while you wonder
if he's noticed when you reel
or stammer. So it's no good pretending
you never liked the shock-streak down your spine
grounding you to the dirt: no, here's to him,
that man, humming like a power line.

Secrets

They're emeralds you daren't wear,
but take out sometimes to hold,
then hide again; they're
white-gold flowers of winter
honeysuckle, forged or
imagined in the heart
or root, sheathed in thin
bark, hidden deep in the branch,
awaiting warmth and damp.
It's December, of course,
and March may never come,
and though you were born rich
and bright, you're not supposed
to share. But sometimes you think
that party will begin, the one with all
the dancing, everyone's stashed
jewels glittering more splendid
and excessive than anyone ever hoped,
and none snatched or smashed by the secret
police. Or maybe there'll be enough
soft days and safe listeners in slow
succession that sometime
your closed throat will believe
in safety and start to loosen,
your tongue will swell
and sparkle like honeysuckle
petals, your lips and fingers
will begin to uncurl and that day,
some day, words will begin to deck
the air gold as pollen, catch
the light like the viridian
flash of stone brought up from

the undermountain black to shine
in daylight. Some day,
you think, maybe you'll
use what you know, tell
what you are, wear your
self bright on your hand or like
a tender bloom in your buttonhole,
and it won't destroy you,
and it won't be held forever against you,
the whole world will forgive and love you.

Legacy

Maybe three of the four grandparents drank,
drank a lot, and it's not much recommendation
if two of them managed to quit, or that you admired
that grit. So maybe the next generation
said, *no way, not me.* And if one has six king-sized bars
of dark chocolate over the fridge, one's shackled
to the Weather Channel, one can't stop shopping, and without
twelve maps, a cooler, and a GPS, one can't travel,
and one embezzled what a dead man left,
and one's always just this side of the hairfine line
marking too many drinks, and one guzzles God
like dry pear wine—still, they're mostly fine,
they're dogged and brave, maybe this stuff dilutes out.
But here you come, and while there hasn't been a real
drunk in thirty years, it's not like you're so much better.
Maybe what's bred in the bone comes out in the Achilles heel.
Maybe you like gin more than is safe,
and are always having to quit for a month, to see if you can,
or at six your spouse calls you at work—*are you ever coming home?*—
or maybe you've an eye for a fetching man,
and maybe you get a lot of your words that way,
getting hooked on someone there's no having,
for a few months, or even a few days.
Maybe, though you're fed full, there's still some craving
eating at you. Maybe family curses stick tight,
and there's a reason DNA looks like links
in the chains that lock you to your crazy acres' walls.
Maybe, one way or another, you'll have your drink.
Maybe you are coming home, sooner than you think.

One More Ars Poetica

They're children of sin who don't know what I did
to get them; don't care if I betrayed
the beloved to steal others' wordsperm, played
the whore whose heart is soft as mallow, cold
as gold. They don't care if Puritans
in the blood, white sails beating
down the thin streams of vein and history,
have snatched up their torches, mob
together under the skin, coming
to burn me for the witch
I am. They'll never debate
all that, righteousness, penitence, shame;
the children of sin are innocent
as their robbed fathers, as their mother's
prey. They babble, laugh, wave
their adorable fingers and toes and lines,
whistle like wrens, coo and splash
in endless summer grass.
And when I'm with them
I'm happy too; with a mother's
utter selfishness, forgetting
the grief and guilt that hung me
a hundred nights in the terrible stocks,
I whisper again in their secret tongue, *my
precious, my loves, don't fear, begin
brave lives, run far, I would do anything
for you, and I have.*

Leaffall

Beauties, this is the bright
and burning hour, time at last
for sailing. Are you glad?
Or are you shivering
in a wind suddenly less
friendly? huddling
with the noisy neighbors, and have they
any comfort to spare
as their slow blood drains down,
withdrawn? In the night
Selene was torn away;
you heard nothing. At noon
Rupert next door cried out
a defiant rustle and leapt:
one gleam, gone. Maybe
he's having the time of his year:
flying, at last! sun
shining through him, ribs
light as light. Maybe
he went into the river,
is growing heavier,
blacker, pickled in cold
brown liquor, all Virginia
tumbling past. Does it
matter? You don't know.
You're all headed the same
way, into utter
change, into what's under
all those leaves
of grass, and though
you know it's the way
it is, can you help

feeling afraid?
Do you cling on
to your mother as the world
rolls downward, darkward?
Have you found
out how to be anything
but young?

Last River

When the souls of the dead kneel down to drink at Lethe
we're startled that it's not more sinister,
but pellucid, amber as autumn ale,
transparent currents starred with yellow leaves,
gray pebbles bright as we thought memory
would always be, the sunlight striking gold
through mossy shallows. There are deer by Lethe,
red hides dappled with the evening light,
forgetting every day the day before
and never missing it. This is a river
with the power of all rivers, only greater,
to let us leave ourselves, let us forget
everything we thought we never could.
This is river, this is broad-brimmed Lethe,
and this is death, and it is beautiful,
so deep and clear that when we've drunk our fill,
some of us ask to stay and go canoeing
down that swift-sliding stream, the way we might
have done once down the Wye or Nanticoke,
when what we wanted most was to forget,
to let our hearts run clean as ribbongrass,
to drink what every deer drinks every day.

In the Graveyard

With the first warmth, the dirt
feels gentler than it has in months,
frost-crumpled, mole-tumbled,
damp-ruffled under the straw-dry
grass under your back. You think
you could lie here forever,
tender as earth under new sun.
But let your mind slide toward sleep and soon
what's hard begins to gouge
through wool and down:
you feel rocks under ribs,
remember again that under
that lovesoft crust are deeps
of running ore, and
gravity, and its iron core.

Seedstash

Shiny, silky, rust-red-brown,
laterally flattened like hungry ticks:
whatever they are, they click
together, an unstrung charm
bracelet, a heap of tiny mouse
castanets. So maybe tonight,
underground, the mice are holding
fiesta, celebrating autumn
or the end of tick season
or the recovery of the Great Mouse
Mother from Lyme. Maybe they stamp
the ground on all fours, again
and again. I doubt they have
tiny mouse sombreros crusted
with silver embroidery, though
I would like that, nor have they sugar
mouse skulls for the Day of the Dead,
unless some bold explorer has stolen
a human one from me. But maybe
with the whisper of their breath
and the slippery click of the seeds,
they take rhythm into their paws and begin
the music; they dip
their claws in a thin vein
of water to make them shine.

Among the Assassins

True bugs, they love
the sunflower stalks
all bristly and thick,
juicy and hairy,
the piecework shadows
of the dahlia leaves,
the falling petals
of the climbing rose.
This year they are
everywhere, efficient,
deadly, peaceful enough
to those of us too large
to eat. The garden is
haunted by conenose,
wheelbug, milkweed
assassin, furled beaks
under every leaf
working both ways,
injecting the venom,
sipping up the melted
guts from inside
after the venom takes,
sweet as a milkshake
made of meat.
Two gray wheel bugs stand
on a sunflower leaf,
one holding a victim,
one considering the offering
like rubies: big enough?
This is love
among the assassins:
the long antennae

spanning the summer
like calipers measuring
an always diminishing
sweetness and heat,
the silky backs' toothed
and bloody gears turning the world.

The Hole

The man on the six-thirty train
began to speak. I tried to look polite.
He said he had been born
with a hole in his heart.
Mm-hmm, I said, regarding my book
with longing. They sewed it up,
he said, when I was a baby.
But now it's back.
Why aren't you dead, I thought
but didn't say. Everything
slips down it, he said.
Blood goes down there
and leaves me trembling.
Sometimes I can hardly stand.
I lost my wife down there,
and she was a big woman,
tall and warm. I edged away
an inch. He didn't follow, just kept on.
My keys, of course, everyone
loses keys, checks, but she
went through and never came back,
like *The Twilight Zone*, that girl
who falls into the wall,
and on the other side nothing
is right. That's some hole, I said
against my will, closing
the book on my finger.
Are you saying your wife
is down by your appendix?
I don't know, he said. But it takes
everything. My aunt said
turn to Jesus, but I think even Jesus

couldn't patch that thing.
Why aren't you dead?
I said it this time.
I don't know, he said
again. I ought to be.
But since I'm not, I get to work
early. The black tunnel
outside rocked and rang.
Aren't you afraid it'll swallow
your job too? I asked.
Yes, he said. But it hasn't yet.
There are those travel forms
in triplicate, the expense accounts,
the grant requests. There are so many,
they take up so much time.
There are more than anyone could finish.
Enough for a thousand
holes, or a million. Why else
would they have all those forms?
The tube lights shone like gas.
Listen, I said.
Why are you talking to me?
I don't know you.
I don't need this.
No, he said, nobody does.

Men's Neckties

They're power nooses choking off
brains from bodies, just enough
to prove a man is something more
than some bright rooster. His top drawer
is civilized and affluent,
in charge, his status bought and spent
on silk, the wormspun ornament.
And yet, the swinging way they hang's . . .
suggestive, don't you think? The things
ties say are all expressed aslant,
but their glance is toward knife-creased pants:
silk arrows pointing down at cocks
that crow through wire and fence and lock.
It's Y, not X, that marks the spot.

Eggcorns

The word *eggcorn* was coined collectively by the linguists . . . someone had written "egg corn" instead of "acorn" . . . [T]he substitution involved more than just ignorance: an acorn is more or less shaped like an egg; and it is a seed, just like grains of corn . . . The crucial element is that the new form makes sense . . . more sense than the original form in many cases.

—CHRIS WAIGL, http://eggcorns.lascribe.net

Making perfect
sense, if different
sense, their young users wonder
hallways, nip problems in the butt,
get past me by a hare's breath.
Eggcorns lighten the daze
of reading and grating: free-raging,
they are liminal, lycanthropic, changing
from the gecko. They are deep-seeded
language disseminating
itself; they are words on the move,
like water hurrying downhill to slack
some internal thirst, but not averse
to a pause on the way
for an eddy, a sudden swirl
to enjoy a mute point
or to party hardy.
And they are what I bring
home to you, who love them
too, who are yourself forever
knew and ongoing as live
language, live water,
try though I do
to take you for granite.

This Time

"Veronica, you know, sometimes in nature things die."
"Not this time!"

—KARL AND VERONICA, PURSUING A (DIFFERENT) HERON

When the fisherman who turned out to be
the cataloging librarian at Wofford
(leading to that surreal pause
exchanging cards mid-river)
saw the heron hobbled from the hook
in its great claw to the lower jaw
of the saber beak, and went to seek
someone to help, and improbably found
the one right person, who sent us
to see what we could do, well, there,
you know, we were. With no right
to think that even with help
we could find the bird, do
what was needed; that it would endure
through clumsy field surgery, or,
surviving, would not be too weak
to hunt, and die there, just too late.
But this was that one time. This time there
by God was the heron, which this time declined
to stab our eyes with its foot of bill; this time
the hook was shallow, the biting line cut,
the wrapped loops scraped free, the folded neck
loosed from hog-tie binding that had held it
strapped to the foot. This time that bird stood up,
clacked its unlocked bill, turned away
its killer's eyes from our intolerable
aid, opened gray wings in some
alien invocation, and caught
flight away. Like grace,

the librarian said, or, I thought, like returning
where I hadn't been this decade, finding
myself remembered, the blessing there
unchanged and unbelievable, oh, yes,
like grace, what you can't earn, like knowing
grace right when you get it, and remembering.

Sirens, Chesapeake Bay

They won't have Hoopers Island, its water-lapped houses;
they cleave to Barren, Bloodsworth, Fox, or Cedar Island;
they love the lonely places, and the men to whom
they sing are also solitary, steering crab-spattered
workboats, pretending to fit a world of water warming
and flooding where no water should belong.
The new-world sirens have no streaming sea-stacks, but are
translated to low needlerush and cord. They steep
their skins in the slip of silt, scour them with sand, and feed
on periwinkles—wrinkled muscles sucked from shell
and rainbow nacre—but they learned their piercing song
from red-winged blackbirds' whistles, ospreys' shrieks, and surf
that hurls its weight upon the beaches' breaking fringes.
Still, sirens do their best work in light airs, slick calm
of noon: the glittering bay lies flat to hear cicadas'
chimes flare up and ring around the shivering song,
which still won't stop the world from doing what it does.
The sirens' sand is going, the islands' peats are sinking;
Hambleton Island's broken into two, and Barren
into three, and Poplar into none. Their feathers
were plucked to deck the muses' broad white brows; the sirens
are half-bird, but they can't fly, half-fish, but they
can't swim; the story says a siren's bound to where
she's set, one island. Aglaope and Ligeia cast their song
from opposite ends of Hambleton the year the narrow
bridge of grassy sand dissolved into a wash of wave.
They cried each other's names, extended arms, and splashed
into the gap; but it had grown too wide. Now each combs
her weedy hair alone; they sing together across
the void, but their wild song's an elegy now, thinner,
more like the wailing of gulls, if all the more seductive
for that (for men love best what's nearly lost). If you

should sail that way, you may think you hear a mere
cormorant-cry, or oystercatchers plashing, but it's Ligeia,
Aglaope, their song of changefulness, and hunger
for one who'll hear their song and answer back in kind.
It's a rare kind of man will do it: one who'll risk
devouring for the sting of that salt knowledge, who knows
erosion, and who'll beach his boat on islands vanishing
under the keel as the wine-dark sea comes rising.

The Man Who Tried to Save Holland Island

2010

A madman, maybe, trying to turn
tide and time from their predestined prey,
with the complication of sea-level rise swift
and hungry on the heels of tide and time.
First there fell peat and persimmon
from where they held their hard ground. Then green
grave-grass gave way, crimped and crumpled
before salt and spartina, as the strait struck
its way west against the wind,
as the cold chop of Chesapeake chewed
at the door. It's there yet, but this year
is the last year for the last house on Holland Island;
this winter it will wash into water and be gone.
And the madman, the man who moved
to save it? who solicited governors, wrote grants,
brought backhoes to drag back from the deep
the dirt that was its due? In ten years who'll know
his name, or what nameless frenzy fretted him
to think this thin strip of grit and grass
could be pulled back, when pelicans plunge
from the brackish branches of the last tree?
Anyone can see it's over.

                                But now how
will it be, fifty years gone, when maybe my own
crazy acres will be battered by breakers
cresting up the Choptank? when the soybean
prairies roll under the wave, when isthmus and island
are awash, and gravestones grate in the surf?

In those end hours, we'll see who'll essay anything
to bring back what's last and lost.
Tell me then who's the madwoman of Wingate,
Wicomico, who curses like the crows at what can't
be changed: tell me who's crazy then.

The Fairy Your Parents Forgot to Ask to the Christening

It was the mosquito fairy, most
beautiful of all in her tiger-striped
stockings: her dainty wings
the prescribed gossamer, her wand
of power a delicate thread
of proboscis, carried in her hand
when she hasn't come to drink,
when she's already flushed
rosy with blood. A bad fairy
to slight and annoy, but, living
inland, they did. And now
her curse flies home to roost on flesh
tender as eyes. Wherever you go, her
minions swarm to your warm
skin. They ignore me, salt-
sullen as the marshmud I was
spawned in, where no one ever forgets
Our Lady of Aedes, or the greenhead fairy,
or the slow spirits of the creeping leech.
Instead they rise straight to you,
strike down their wands into your pink
champagne veins, drawn
to what your parents begot
and forgot, the sweetness which once
drew them too, whining
their buzz of delight
and spite as they drink you dry.

Promise Land

They've never seen it spelled,
I guess, only heard it said
in church: so when they write
it down, the Promised Land,
heaven, becomes this other
thing, the Promise Land. Their heaven
is the land of promises, where
eternal checks are always in the mail
and every morning finds us in the gym.
Where those jeans, you swear, make me look small.
Where of course Monsanto doesn't plot
to own each seed of every spear of corn.
Where your senators read your mail. Where
we'll see the beloved dead again, and never wish
we hadn't. And it's the land where you and I
can each admire and like and love the other
forever, forever, I promise, forever.

Secret Identity

Wonder Woman can't spin like a cyclone
and burst into thunderstars
when Steve's watching. Who wants to know
his yeoman could break him in two?
If Clark and Diana and Bruce
were something more, Lois and Steve
and Vicki never knew.
Especially Steve, who needed Diana
Prince to pick up his dry cleaning,
polish his shoes.
Diana, the Incredibles are two
generations away—and even they
forget they're married
to power. Nor are you
an X-man, to enjoy perpetual youth,
always someone else
to wash the tights (we never see who),
always other mutants handy to talk to,
to wear fire or lightning
on their hands like electric tattoos.
This is the world you knew,
the story that ends
in silence. So you
take your strength, your speed,
your fraught gift and slow fuse
to the streets, where
the wrong people praise
you blindly, admire the bruises
you give them.
Daylight hides what you are;
you have to choose.
You may be loved, but no one
will see you all the way through,

know all your names, and who
can you blame, why
would they want to?
Even your mother has
a paradise to run. No matter
if the person you want most to admire
your flashing shackles is the one who'll refuse
to know their power as yours:
there is no truth
you could tell that would change this;
when it comes to love, that glittering
lasso is no use.

Cannibal Family

> Be praised, my Lord, through our Sister Death,
> from whose embrace no living person can escape.
>
> —ST. FRANCIS OF ASSISI, "CANTICLE OF THE SUN"

> We be of one blood, thou and I.
>
> —RUDYARD KIPLING, "KAA'S HUNTING"

Sister Wolf is easy to love, when I have no flocks.
Mother Osprey with her imperial face
and implacable eye—anyone would claim her,
anyone but Cousin Croaker
thrashing his muscled pewter
spine in the clutch of her claw.
Even Uncle Slug trailing his silver ribbons
is no slimier than anyone's heart.
But this is the world
where we eat our family, our own,
or else fall prey too soon
to those gentle nephews, the segmented worms,
or Aunt Necrophila, always affectionate
in her black and saffron jacket.
So, Grandmother Cornbread,
how fine your flavor, all grit and salt,
how you taste of the sun and the bees,
the leafhoppers poisoned to bring you to me,
the tender deer who died for wanting you.
Kale, third cousin once removed,
how beautiful your emerald
ruffles, like a Spanish dancer's skirt;
how the tang of vinegar brings out the savor
of the strong green blood that in another
bite we will share. And you, Brother Deer
Tick, whose infected mandibles changed
my blood, inflamed my joints,

swelled thumbs and knees knobby and round
as worlds themselves: you are part of me
now, with me to the end, indeed
we are of one blood, you and I.

Eating the Dead

We ate him one transparent
winter noon, clear-bare.
He sparkled in a glass
vial that his heir
brought from the shed to share.
"Recognize it?" asked his son,
my father. "Calcium
carbonate," I guessed
from the coarse off-white grit.
He nodded, shook out the gray
grains till the jar was done—
fragments of tooth and bone,
the softer flakes of flesh
burnt, compressed and wrung—
and passed them to his heir
apparent, to eat ash
while the vial lit
its empty shaft with sun.
The truth is we both wished
his heart or gut could stay
in us; we didn't want
one fleck to go to waste.
We licked him off our palms,
legator, father: gone
in a lick of dust,
a flash of tongue.

The People She Knows

She says she knows so few,
though she's lived here fifty years.
No one wants to level or paint
or re-wire the walls; she's not
from around here. But take her
walking, all that changes. The oak
with no new growth: *what's wrong?*
she asks it, *come on,* she pleads.
Don't ask whether it tells her, or how.
Crossing the sparkling thread of Line
Ditch, she holds a muscled ironwood bole
which steadies her like a human arm.
The frogs in the little marsh had names; so
had the water snake who ate them
all, and was not blamed. The sybil tree
frog calls, forecasting, she says, rain at last.
When we lay her under the sand,
here will be around her: all the people
she knows, the thin roots bringing back
the deep dirt lightward, the black
blot of buzzard poised to offer transformation,
the whispered, crumbly words of worm.

The Body

Children of the night, shut up!
—*Love at First Bite,* STAN DRAGOTI (DIRECTOR),
ROBERT KAUFMAN (AUTHOR), 1979

All day the body is servant
and mistress, vessel
and vehicle: we comb
its hair against the grain,
wrap it in fashion, walk it
like a dog, hide its cellulite.
At night it is itself, no one's
vessel or pair of hands; the body
wears shapeless flannel, gives
up on beauty for one more night,
and, if we're lucky, gives
sweet sleep, the falling-
still of all those voices,
the children of the day
who never shut up.
The body tonight is a creature
of darkness, barefoot, peaceably
monstrous in its lair:
Dracula in his soft coffin,
or the swamp monster at home
having cocoa, watching the soaps.
Here I am, child of the night.
My flannels don't match,
my fat hangs out,
I have let go of all
the things I wanted all day,
and I am already escaping you
into what no one can say.

Swarm

Twenty-five years back, at home,
the summer hour was late when the afternoon
light began to hum, and a thousand
specks came arrowing out of the west,
the air waxed thick with honeybees up in swarm.
They crept and crawled on our closed
screens, stormed and boomed around the old
maple: one of the things you remember
forever, a sign you can't read, alien,
and yet down in your bones you know
you want this. Want to open the screen and go
out there, breathe the hot wind of gauze
wings, caress striped velvet, feel
the sisters' feet prick your skin.
I didn't know then that swarming
bees don't sting, and working bees hardly
sting, and bumblebees let you stroke
their black satin as they drink the blooms.
I didn't know how little harm
most things mean, how even the dangerous
snake tries to slide away, how safe
we were. But I think of it now, stirring
barehand the soft bees, shaking
down this week's singing swarm,
hoping they'll come home. The summer
hour is late, but not too late.

Printed in the USA
CPSIA information can be obtained
at www.ICGtesting.com
LVHW041530070924
790346LV00001B/85